Contents

Introduction

Artificial intelligence was once seen in pop culture as something almost magical that had far-reaching impacts that were often negative. Movies and series such as 2001: Space Odyssey, Terminator, The Matrix and Star Trek all demonstrated various scenarios of how AI can impact humans. It is interesting to see how each of these cases of pop culture has manifested into today's reality. Space exploration and exploration of our own world is being propelled by AI that learns how to navigate its environment with more dexterity than its human counterparts. At the time of this writing, a company called Neuralink is developing brain implants to help individuals who have suffered strokes or have ALS to communicate via thought. New York City entertained using AI powered robots for both police and fire departments in 2023 and digital twinning is not quite a holodeck, but it does utilize AI to help with engineering and prototyping efforts in a more interactive manner that can be more cost effective.

In all these scenarios, fictional and otherwise, AI is a tool that aids humans in performing tasks. This is one of the most important takeaways in this primer. AI is a tool that when properly managed and governed can aid humans significantly. Like any tool, to get the most benefit from it, one must be properly trained and use the tool in proper context with appropriate safeguards. Even the humble hammer abides by this axiom. Owning a hammer does not make one a carpenter but for a carpenter to be successful they must own one and be trained with it. AI is similar. Implementing AI systems does not guarantee success but implementing them poorly almost certainly guarantees failure.

One way to mitigate the risk of poor AI implementations is to adhere to frameworks and standards that address key areas of deployment and management. These frameworks help senior management and subject matter experts deploy AI in an ethical manner and help guard against failures and mitigate risks that may arise during the lifecycle of an AI implementation. Good frameworks have several key components:

Broadly applicable – Frameworks should be applicable to most of the scenarios within the framework's scope.

Widely available and understood – Frameworks, whether at company level or an industry level, should be presented in a way that is easy to understand and that makes the material of the framework accessible to all who are subject to using it.

Flexible – Frameworks should provide a wireframe for what needs to be in place while allowing organizations that use the frameworks to tailor the application to meet specific needs.

AI is currently moving at breakneck pace as are the standards that are being developed to help govern it. This primer is meant to be a starting point to help organizations develop governance by leveraging some of the emerging standards. By doing so, organizations are preparing themselves for potential regulations and mitigating potential risks. More importantly, organizations will be setting themselves up for more successful and ethical AI implementations in an environment that is demonstrating AI is competitive advantage.

Brief history of AI

The pursuit of contemporary AI started in the 1950's. It started as a summer workshop amongst academics and is now estimated to have a market size of more than one trillion dollars by 2030. The following is a brief description of the history that got us from an academic workshop in the 1950's to an economic juggernaut that has a permanent and far-reaching impact on society today.

In 1956, John McCarthy, Marvin Minsky, Nathaniel Rochester, and Claude Shannon organized the Dartmouth Summer Research Project on Artificial Intelligence, which is widely regarded as the birthplace of AI. At the conference, they proposed the creation of "thinking machines" that could learn, reason, and make decisions like humans. The applications developed in the years to follow were considered amazing at the time. Computers were solving algebra problems and learning to speak English. The tasks once thought to be the providence of intelligent beings were being replicated with programs.

In the early to mid-1960s, funding for AI projects began to take place. The Defense Advanced Research Projects Agency (DARPA) provided several million dollars a year until 1970. One of the more notable breakthroughs during this period was the development of "micro-worlds' where the rules of physics were articulated with simplified models to better understand and work with foundational principles. This research began the work in machine vision by a research team led by Gerald Sussman.

In the 1970s, AI began facing setbacks. Researchers were beginning to realize that a tremendous amount of computing power and data would be required to make significant progress in the field. Financial backers at DARPA were becoming frustrated with the lack of progress in the field and began cancelling projects in the field. The National Academies of Science and Engineering, after spending $20 million in funding over a decade, also ended its support. This ushered in a period that is called the AI Winter when all advancement in the field was frozen.

In the early 1980's, another boost to the AI field took place in the form of expert systems. These systems used data compiled for domain experts to arrive at solutions to queries or problems through a set of defined rules.

With business funding AI projects, supporting industries in hardware and software began to emerge to meet the demand. This started the knowledge revolution and the development of what are called knowledge-based systems.

Early knowledge-based systems were to suffer the same fate as early AI systems in the late 80s and early 90s. The hardware and software required to run these systems became expensive and the cost outpaced the value. The systems that were developed were only viable for very specific context. Organizations began defunding AI projects, and the field suffered another period of frozen investment.

Starting in the early 21st century, AI began to re-emerge and hasn't stopped since. New techniques, such as backward propagation, were being implemented into neural networks to make them more viable models. The explosion of the internet provided for the development of data and processing power that is needed to develop effective AI, and the democratization of AI through open-source tools has allowed many bright and talented groups to contribute to a rapidly expanding group of practitioners.

We are now in an era of AI where machines can perform tasks once thought to be accomplished only by humans. In addition to beating humans in complex games such as chess and Go, machines are learning to speak, drive, and even create new things using generative AI. The tools that are now available to apply AI-driven solutions are available to almost anyone with a computer and internet connection. In the next section, we will go over some more formal definitions of AI in more detail and provide some high-level information on the kinds of AI models available today.

Overview of AI

AI is a term that covers a great number of technologies and capabilities. There are currently considered to be three tiers of AI:

Artificial Narrow Intelligence (ANI) - ANI is designed to perform a specific task or solve a specific problem. Examples include voice assistants like Siri and Alexa, which can understand and respond to specific voice commands, and image recognition systems used in security cameras and self-driving cars. This is the current stage of our AI capabilities and is the focus of this primer and is what is referred to when this primer mentions AI.

Artificial General Intelligence (AGI) - AGI is designed to perform any intellectual task that a human can do. AGI systems can reason, plan, learn, and adapt to new situations, and can perform multiple tasks across different domains. AGI systems do not yet exist, and research in this area is ongoing. Many GPT (Generative Pre-Trained Transformer) models are seen to be the first steps on this journey.

Artificial Super Intelligence (ASI) - ASI is a hypothetical AI system that surpasses human intelligence in every domain and can learn and improve itself exponentially. While ASI is not yet a reality, it is a topic of discussion in AI research and raises important ethical and societal questions about the role of AI in our lives. An entity that is a hyper enhanced reflection of the various facets of its creator (us) is as much a scientific discussion as it is philosophical one.

Within artificial intelligence there are several different subsets of tools and capabilities. Deep learning and machine learning are topics that are often used to describe these components of artificial intelligence. The figure below is one that is commonly shown to describe the interplay of these concepts.

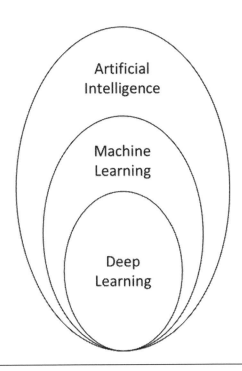

Artificial Intelligence (AI)	Broad field that focuses on creating intelligent machines that can mimic human thought processes and decision-making. AI systems can be designed to perform specific tasks, such as recognizing speech, optimizing resources, or identifying objects in images.
Machine Learning (ML)	Subset of AI that involves training algorithms to learn patterns in data, without being explicitly programmed. ML algorithms use statistical techniques to automatically improve their performance over time, based on the feedback they receive from the data they analyze. Common examples of ML applications include recommendation systems, fraud detection, and image and speech recognition.
Deep Learning (DL)	Subset of ML that uses neural networks, which are layered networks of interconnected nodes that simulate the behavior of the human brain, to analyze and extract patterns from data. DL algorithms can learn and improve their performance with large amounts of data and can be used for complex tasks such as natural language processing and image and video recognition.

Types of learning

In addition to the types of AI, there are different ways in which AI "learns." There are several different types of learning in the context of machine learning. These learning methods are driven by the algorithm, available data, and objective of the AI.

Reinforcement Learning	Supervised Learning	Unsupervised Learning
Reinforcement learning (RL) is a type of machine learning where an AI agent learns to make decisions by interacting with an environment, receiving feedback in the form of rewards or punishments based on its actions. The goal of RL is to learn a policy that maximizes the cumulative reward over time.	Supervised learning is a type of machine learning where an AI algorithm is trained on a labeled dataset, meaning that each example in the dataset is paired with a known label or target value. The algorithm learns to make predictions based on the input features of the data, and the known labels are used to guide the learning process.	Unsupervised learning is a type of machine learning where an AI algorithm is trained on an unlabeled dataset, meaning that the data does not have any known labels or target values. The goal of unsupervised learning is to discover patterns or structure in the data, without being explicitly told what to look for.
robotics, game playing, and optimization problems	image classification, speech recognition, and sentiment analysis	clustering, dimensionality reduction, and anomaly detection

AI models

AI models are also broadly categorized into classification models or regression models. Some models can perform both functions just as some models can be categorized as having more than one learning method.

Classification models use data features to draw a conclusion on what the data is describing (the label). Providing image input to a model and having the model label the image as a cat or dog is an example of classification model. Some models can provide more than one classification from the features along with the probability that the classification is correct.

Regression models provide predictions of values based upon historical data provided to the model to train it. Simple linear and multiple linear regression models are commonly known but additional machine learning models are available.

New models are continuously being researched and many sophisticated AI systems use a combination of models. This primer is not a practitioners guide for model development, but the following table provides a list of the more common models and how they are classified to give the reader a high-level familiarity with common models that may appear in an environment leveraging AI.

Model	Description	Deep Learning	Classification	Regression	Reinforcement	Supervised	Unsupervised
Linear Regression	Used to model the relationship between a dependent variable and one or more independent variables. It assumes a linear relationship between the variables and predicts the value of the dependent variable based on the values of the independent variables.			X		X	
Logistic Regression	Used to predict the probability of an event occurring based on a set of input variables. It is commonly used for classification tasks, where the goal is to predict a binary or categorical outcome.		X			X	
Decision Trees	Used for both regression and classification tasks. They recursively split the data into subsets based on the values of the input variables and build a tree-like model that can be used to make predictions.		X	X		X	
Random Forest	Combines multiple decision trees to improve the accuracy and robustness of the model. It is commonly used for classification and regression tasks and can handle large datasets with high-dimensional input variables.		X	X		X	
Naive Bayes	Probabilistic machine learning algorithm used for classification tasks. It assumes that the input variables are independent of each other and predicts the probability of a class label based on the joint probability of the input variables.		X			X	
k-Nearest Neighbors (k-NN)	used for classification and regression tasks. It predicts the value of a new data point based on the k nearest data points in the training set.		X	X		X	X
Support Vector Machines (SVM)	Used for classification and regression tasks. It finds the optimal hyperplane that separates the data into different classes and can handle high-dimensional input variables.		X	X		X	X
Ensemble Methods	Ensemble methods are machine learning algorithms that combine multiple models to improve the accuracy and robustness of the model. Examples of ensemble methods include bagging, boosting, and stacking.		X	X		X	
Gradient Boosting	Ensemble learning algorithm that combines multiple weak learners to improve the accuracy of the model. It iteratively adds new decision trees to the model to correct the errors of the previous trees.		X	X		X	

Model	Description	Deep Learning	Classification	Regression	Reinforcement	Supervised	Unsupervised
Recurrent Neural Networks (RNN)	Neural networks are commonly used in natural language processing and speech recognition tasks. They use recurrent layers to process sequences of input data and can learn to predict the next element in a sequence based on the previous elements.	X	X	X		X	
Long Short-Term Memory (LSTM)	Type of RNN designed to address the problem of vanishing gradients in traditional RNNs. They use memory cells to store and retrieve information over long time periods and can learn to model complex temporal patterns in the data.	X	X	X		X	
Generative Adversarial Networks (GAN)	Neural networks used for generating new data that resembles training data. They consist of two networks, a generator network that creates new data, and a discriminator network that evaluates the quality of the generated data.	X	Generative Model			X	
Autoencoders	Neural networks are used for data compression and feature extraction. They consist of an encoder network that compresses the input data into a lower dimensional representation, and a decoder network that reconstructs the original data from the compressed representation.	X	X	X			X
Deep Belief Networks (DBN)	Neural network used for unsupervised learning tasks, such as clustering and dimensionality reduction. They consist of multiple layers of restricted Boltzmann machines, which are a type of unsupervised learning algorithm.	X	X	X			X
Restricted Boltzmann Machines (RBM)	Learning algorithm used for feature learning and dimensionality reduction. They are used in deep belief networks and can learn to represent the input data in a lower-dimensional space.	X	X	X			X
Deep Reinforcement Learning (DRL)	Reinforcement learning algorithm that uses deep neural networks to learn policies for decision-making tasks. It has been successfully used in game playing, robotics, and other complex tasks where a large amount of state information is available.	X	Neither				

Each model listed provides distinct capabilities as well as distinct challenges to organizations. The management of an AI-enabled environment can quickly become messy. Data, variables, tests, and metrics can be unique for each model which makes a prescriptive standard for each model difficult to maintain at an organizational level.

The AI lifecycle

The lifecycle for AI is not too dissimilar from the software development lifecycle. Many for-profit and non-for-profit organizations have developed numerous depictions of AI lifecycles with varying degrees of detail. A common theme is plan, design, build, deploy, test, and monitor. The approach is iterative in nature. As AI models begin deteriorating or drifting, or better data becomes available, the process begins anew.

Plan: In this stage, the aim is to understand the problem at hand and determine if an AI-based solution is appropriate. This involves defining clear objectives and success metrics. Key tasks in this phase include identifying data sources, feasibility analysis, and defining resource needs. It's crucial to align the AI project objectives with overall business goals and understand any legal or ethical implications of the proposed solution.

Design: In this phase, the architecture and model of the AI solution are designed. This includes designing the overall system architecture, selecting the AI techniques to be used (e.g., machine learning, deep learning, natural language processing, etc.), and planning for data collection and processing. Depending on the complexity of the project, multiple AI techniques might be used in combination.

Build: This phase is where the AI models are developed and trained. It starts with data collection, cleaning, and preprocessing, followed by feature extraction and selection. Then the AI models are trained using the prepared data, which often involves iterative experimentation to optimize the models. This phase also includes developing the necessary software and infrastructure to support the AI models.

Test: In this phase, the AI system is thoroughly tested to ensure it works as expected and achieves the defined objectives. This involves both functional testing (does the system perform its intended function?) and non-functional testing (how does the system perform under different conditions?). Additionally, the system's performance is benchmarked against the success metrics defined in the planning stage.

Deploy: Once the models are trained and validated, they are deployed into the production environment. This might involve integrating the models into existing software systems, setting up application programming interfaces (API) endpoints for model predictions, and preparing the infrastructure to support the production models. It's important to have a robust deployment process to ensure the models can operate reliably and scale to handle the intended workload.

Monitor: After deployment, the AI system needs to be continuously monitored to ensure it continues to perform well. This includes monitoring system performance, data quality, and model accuracy. AI systems can drift over time as the underlying data changes, so it's important to regularly retrain or fine-tune the models as needed. Monitoring also includes checking for any unexpected or undesirable behavior from the AI system and implementing corrective measures if needed.

Example:

A company in New York is planning to revolutionize its hiring process by implementing a resume screening system that performs rankings of candidates that is augmented by an online multiple-choice test that assesses if the candidate is a good fit for the company's culture.

For the **planning phase**, process owners and subject matters drive the conversation of what is needed, and engineers and data scientists can drive the conversation of what is possible. Gaps between the two are then discussed and direction for the solution can begin. Legal and ethical issues are reviewed as well.

During the legal review, it has been discovered that hiring systems based on AI that are implemented in New York City require annual bias audits. The company thinks this is a good practice and develops requirements in the planning phase that will facilitate ongoing audits.

The **design phase** becomes more technical in nature but still requires input from business owners. Team members from human resources are a part of the design team and participate in discussions. An agile method is being used for development so sprints of design, build, test are being used for more interactive input from subject matter experts. Data is of paramount importance for AI, so data owners and data scientists are integral as well.

Build occurs using the hardware and software platforms decided upon in earlier phases. The current company is large enough to support an internal build without vendor licensing for third-party solutions. Models are built using standard open-source software that is supported by a large enough talent pool internally and externally.

Testing occurs after each sprint. Test scripts were developed during the design phase and are executed by developers and then by functional subject matter experts. Test results are documented, and exceptions are fed into the design phase for the next build. Human resources and hiring managers use the interface and test the results against passed hiring decisions. Since bias and fairness is a core ethical principle for the company as well as legal requirement, statistical reviews of demographic data that pertains to candidates are reviewed. It was found in one review that first and last name drove bias in selection, so the features were removed as inputs into the model.

Once the AI build is completed to the satisfaction of all parties, signoffs are obtained, and the solution is **deployed** in accordance with deployment plan. Ample instruction and training are provided for users both internal and external.

The system is **monitored** for results as well as usability. During the initial couple of weeks, applicants were having issues with some of the testing questions. The feedback gathered from an email inbox dedicated to raising issues captured the concerns which then turned into requirements. Additionally, HR managers were noticing some trends of bias in ethnicity. The team discovered zip code was inadvertently driving some biasness in selection and the feature was removed in the next model update.

During each phase in the example, various controls points existed. The controls helped to keep the AI system governed and managed while meeting the organizations objectives and remaining ethical. The next sections will touch more upon controls as they relate to AI and governance.

Governance

Governance refers to the systems and processes by which a company is directed and controlled. It forms the framework for attaining a company's objectives and encompasses practically every sphere of management, from action plans and internal controls to performance measurement and corporate disclosure. In essence, corporate governance involves balancing the interests of a company's many stakeholders, such as shareholders, management, customers, suppliers, financiers, government, and the community.

Given the critical importance of investor trust in maintaining a company's value, corporate governance practices focus heavily on ensuring transparency, accountability, and security in a company's relationship with its stakeholders. A robust corporate governance framework establishes the roles and responsibilities of each participant in the corporation. This includes the board of directors, management, and shareholders. Good corporate governance procedures are those that motivate the management to perform at its best and act in the shareholders' interest.

Key principles that underpin good corporate governance include fairness, transparency, accountability, and responsibility. Fairness ensures equal treatment of all stakeholders. Transparency refers to the clear, timely, and accurate communication of a company's financial performance and business activities. Accountability ensures that management is answerable to the board, and the board, in turn, is accountable to the shareholders. Responsibility pertains to the legal and ethical obligations of the corporation towards its stakeholders and society at large.

Governance is usually articulated through policies, standards, and procedures developed by the organization and owned by individuals that are responsible for implementing processes and controls to ensure governance is executed properly. Reviews performed by parties internal and/or external to the organization but independent of the processes help assure senior management and other stakeholders that the execution of the policies, standards, and procedures is occurring as designed within the framework and that the controls in place are operating effectively.

Roles and responsibilities

Within an organization, the governance of AI includes roles and responsibilities that span various departments and levels. It's not just about technology or data. AI governance involves considering ethical, legal, and societal implications in addition to technology. A monitoring and control framework to ensure compliance and monitoring is executed is also a key component of governance. Roles and responsibilities can vary depending on the size, sector, and AI maturity of the organization but in all cases, the governance of AI should be a cross-functional effort involving a wide range of stakeholders.

Leadership Team (CEO, Board of Directors, Executive Management) sets the overall strategic direction for AI in the organization. They communicate the organization's vision for AI, ensuring that it aligns with the organization's core values and complies with legal obligations. Moreover, they are instrumental in fostering a corporate culture that emphasizes ethical AI use, promoting responsible behaviors throughout the organization.

Chief AI Officer/Chief Data Officer oversees the strategic deployment of AI within the organization and ensures the quality, integrity, and security of the data used in AI applications. They are expected to advocate for ethical AI practices and work with various departments to integrate AI into the broader business strategy. They often become the bridge connecting technological possibilities and business goals.

Functional Owners are subject matter experts responsible for the domain in which the AI is used. This group provides critical input into the design and testing of AI implementations. Their approval signifies that the AI is built in accordance with the needs of the organization and that all testing requirements have been successfully met.

AI Ethics Board/Committee is responsible for developing and updating ethical guidelines for AI use. They monitor the organization's adherence to these guidelines, evaluate the ethical implications of AI projects, and ensure corrective actions are taken when necessary. Additionally, they have a role in educating all employees about ethical AI use to promote a culture of responsible AI within the organization.

AI Project Managers/Leaders align AI projects with the organization's strategic goals and ethical guidelines. They coordinate cross-functional teams, manage project progress, risks, and resources, and facilitate effective communication among all project stakeholders. Their leadership ensures the successful execution of AI projects.

AI Developers and Engineers are on the front lines of building and maintaining the organization's AI systems. They are required to follow organizational policies and ethical guidelines, emphasizing fairness, transparency, and security in the AI systems they develop. Regular testing and updating of these systems ensure their reliability and performance.

Data Governance Team ensures the privacy, quality, and security of the data used in AI systems. They implement data management and governance frameworks and liaise with legal and compliance teams on data-related regulatory matters. They also balance data access needs with privacy and security considerations.

Legal and Compliance Team provides essential guidance on legal and regulatory matters related to AI. They help monitor compliance with relevant laws and regulations, assess potential legal risks in AI projects, and work with other teams to ensure legal and regulatory considerations are integrated into the organization's AI usage.

HR and Training Teams critical role in developing and delivering training programs related to AI ethics and responsible AI use. They incorporate AI considerations into recruitment, evaluation, and employee development processes, fostering an innovative and learning-oriented culture around AI.

Internal Audit Team ensures compliance with internal AI policies and external regulations. They conduct audits of AI practices, assess associated risks, and provide recommendations for improving the governance and management of AI within the organization. Their work provides essential oversight, enhancing the organization's AI practices.

Policies, standards, and procedures

When it comes to the governance of AI, policies, standards, and procedures play crucial roles in guiding and regulating its development, deployment, and use. Together, these elements help organizations foster responsible and trustworthy AI practices, mitigate risks, and ensure alignment with legal, ethical, and social considerations. Here's how they differ in the context of AI governance:

AI policies set the overarching principles, objectives, and ethical considerations that govern the organization's approach to AI. They establish the values and goals to be pursued while deploying AI systems. AI policies may address issues such as transparency, fairness, accountability, privacy, and bias mitigation. These policies provide a strategic direction and ensure that AI aligns with the organization's values and societal expectations.

Policies may have several different components and vary with the needs and complexity of the organization. When crafting a policy to address AI, other policy templates within an organization should be reviewed. Existing policies will provide guidance on how to articulate policy elements that should already exist in an organization such as policy purpose, escalation, policy owner, roles, and responsibilities, etc. Following are policy elements that may be in addition to existing policy elements when developing governance for AI:

Ethical Principles: AI policies often include a set of ethical principles that guide the organization's AI practices. These principles may encompass values such as fairness, transparency, accountability, privacy, safety, and human-centricity. They serve as a foundation for ensuring that AI technologies are developed and used in a manner that aligns with societal norms and values.

Governance Framework: The policy may outline a governance framework that defines the structures, roles, and responsibilities for overseeing AI activities within the organization. This includes identifying key stakeholders, establishing accountability mechanisms, and determining decision-making processes for AI-related initiatives.

Regulatory Compliance: AI policies should address compliance with applicable laws, regulations, and industry standards. They may outline specific legal and regulatory requirements related to data protection, privacy, discrimination, intellectual property, and consumer protection. The policy should ensure that AI systems and practices adhere to these legal and regulatory obligations.

17

Transparency and Explainability: Given the potential opacity of AI systems, policies often emphasize the importance of transparency and explainability. This component highlights the organization's commitment to providing clear explanations of AI decisions, disclosing the use of AI technologies, and promoting understandable and interpretable AI models and algorithms.

Data Governance: AI policies typically address data governance practices, including data collection, storage, quality, and security. This component may establish guidelines for responsible data management, data sharing, data anonymization, and consent mechanisms. It may also address issues related to bias, fairness, and the use of sensitive or personal data.

Risk Assessment and Mitigation: Policies may include a framework for assessing and mitigating risks associated with AI. This involves identifying potential risks and harms, conducting impact assessments, implementing risk management strategies, and establishing mechanisms for ongoing monitoring and evaluation of AI systems' performance and impact.

Training and Awareness: Policies may highlight the importance of training employees and stakeholders on AI-related topics. They may include provisions for raising awareness about AI technologies, promoting responsible AI use, and ensuring that employees have the necessary skills and knowledge to work with AI systems safely and ethically.

Stakeholder Involvement: AI policies may encourage collaboration with external stakeholders, such as academic institutions, industry partners, and civil society organizations. This component promotes knowledge sharing, research partnerships, and cooperation to address common challenges and advance responsible AI practices.

AI standards are guidelines, specifications, or frameworks that define the technical requirements and best practices for developing, deploying, and managing AI systems. They establish benchmarks and ensure that AI technologies meet specific criteria related to safety, security, reliability, and interoperability. Standards may cover aspects like data quality, model validation, explainability, robustness, and compliance with regulatory requirements. Adhering to AI standards helps organizations maintain quality, mitigate risks, and foster trust in AI technologies.

AI standards consist of various components that provide guidelines, specifications, and benchmarks for the development, deployment, and management of AI systems. These components collectively form the foundation for ensuring quality, reliability, and responsible development and use of AI systems. AI standards provide organizations with a common reference point, enabling them to meet industry best practices, enhance interoperability, mitigate risks, and build trust in AI technologies. While specific components may vary depending on the standard and its focus, here are some key elements commonly found:

Terminology and Definitions: AI standards often include a section that establishes common terminology and definitions to ensure clarity and consistency in communication and understanding across different stakeholders and organizations. This component helps create a shared language for discussing AI-related concepts and technologies.

Technical Requirements: AI standards specify the technical requirements that AI systems should meet to ensure quality, reliability, and safety. This component may cover aspects such as data quality and preprocessing, model development and evaluation, algorithm selection and validation, system architecture, interoperability, and performance metrics. It provides guidelines for implementing AI technologies effectively.

Model Validation and Evaluation: AI standards often outline methodologies and criteria for validating and evaluating AI models. This component may include guidelines for data selection, cross-validation techniques, performance metrics, benchmarking, and statistical analysis. It helps ensure that AI models are accurate, reliable, and robust.

Data Governance and Management: AI standards may provide guidelines for data governance and management practices. This component covers topics such as data collection, storage, preprocessing, anonymization, consent mechanisms, and data protection. It ensures that organizations handle data responsibly and adhere to relevant privacy and security requirements.

19

Interoperability and Compatibility: Standards may address interoperability and compatibility aspects of AI systems. This component defines guidelines for data formats, APIs (Application Programming Interfaces), data sharing protocols, and system integration. It facilitates the seamless exchange of data and interoperability among AI systems.

Testing and Validation Procedures: AI standards often include procedures and methodologies for testing and validating AI systems. This component outlines recommended testing frameworks, test cases, and evaluation procedures to assess the performance, reliability, and safety of AI technologies. It helps ensure that AI systems meet the specified requirements and perform as intended.

Documentation and Reporting: Standards may include requirements for documentation and reporting. This component defines the necessary documentation to accompany AI systems, such as model documentation, technical specifications, user manuals, and reporting templates. It promotes transparency and facilitates understanding and communication about AI systems.

AI procedures are the detailed step-by-step instructions or processes that dictate how specific AI-related tasks or activities should be carried out within the organization. They outline the methodologies, tools, and guidelines for implementing AI systems. AI procedures may cover aspects such as data collection and preprocessing, algorithm selection and training, testing and validation, monitoring and maintenance, and incident response. By following these procedures, organizations can ensure consistency, reliability, and compliance throughout the AI lifecycle.

AI procedures consist of detailed step-by-step instructions, processes, and guidelines that dictate how specific tasks and activities related to artificial intelligence should be carried out within an organization. These procedures help ensure consistency, efficiency, and compliance in the implementation, management, and maintenance of AI systems. These components collectively provide detailed instructions and guidelines for executing AI-related tasks and activities. AI procedures help ensure consistent, reliable, and compliant implementation, management, and maintenance of AI systems while promoting good practices and reducing potential risks. Key components commonly found in AI procedures:

Task Description: Each AI procedure begins with a clear description of the task or activity it covers. This component provides an overview of the specific objective or outcome the procedure aims to achieve. It helps stakeholders understand the purpose and scope of the procedure.

Roles and Responsibilities: AI procedures define the roles and responsibilities of individuals involved in executing the tasks. This component specifies who is responsible for each step, clarifies their roles, and highlights any dependencies or coordination required between different stakeholders. It ensures accountability and clear communication within the organization.

Step-by-Step Instructions: The core component of AI procedures is the step-by-step instructions. This section outlines the sequence of actions, activities, or processes that need to be followed to complete the task successfully. It provides a detailed roadmap for executing the task, ensuring consistency and accuracy in the implementation of AI systems.

Tools and Resources: Procedures often specify the tools, software, hardware, or resources required to carry out the tasks effectively. This component ensures that the necessary infrastructure, software frameworks, programming languages, or datasets are available for the execution of AI-related activities. It helps stakeholders understand the prerequisites and dependencies of the procedure.

Data Collection and Preprocessing: AI procedures may include guidelines for data collection and preprocessing. This component outlines the methods, sources, and quality requirements for acquiring relevant data. It may cover aspects such as data sampling, data cleaning, feature engineering, and data labeling, ensuring that the collected data is suitable for training and validating AI models.

Model Development and Training: Procedures related to model development and training provide guidance on selecting appropriate algorithms, model architectures, and training methodologies. This component outlines the steps for model training, hyperparameter tuning, cross-validation, and performance evaluation. It ensures consistency and reproducibility in the model development process.

Testing and Validation: AI procedures may include instructions for testing and validating AI models or systems. This component outlines the methodologies and metrics for evaluating the performance, accuracy, and robustness of the AI system. It may cover techniques such as unit testing, integration testing, model validation, and model evaluation against predefined benchmarks.

Monitoring and Maintenance: Procedures often address the monitoring and maintenance of AI systems. This component defines the metrics to be monitored, the frequency of monitoring, and the processes for detecting anomalies or performance degradation. It may also include instructions for updating models, retraining, or fine-tuning the system based on new data or changing requirements.

Incident Response and Troubleshooting: Procedures may include guidelines for incident response and troubleshooting in the event of system failures, errors, or unintended consequences. This component outlines the steps to be followed to identify the issue, isolate the problem, and resolve it efficiently. It helps minimize downtime and mitigate potential risks.

Documentation and Reporting: AI procedures often emphasize the importance of documentation and reporting. This component specifies the required documentation for each step of the procedure, such as code documentation, model documentation, and result reporting. It ensures transparency, traceability, and knowledge transfer within the organization.

This set of guidance works in a certain hierarchy. Policies usually dictate the need for standards that should be present, and standards will require procedures that instruct a user on how to execute steps in processes that follow a standard.

We can use a software development lifecycle (SDLC) scenario as an example. A corporate policy may require that all software development activities adhere to a set of testing standards that produce test results approved by users. The standards could indicate which tests are appropriate for specified systems or which systems must be used.

22

Procedures could describe the detailed execution and instruction of the testing and describe more details such as where results are stored or what specific signoffs are required. These documents may have more than a one-to-one relationship. Continuing with our SDLC example, both data and SDLC policy may be reflected and referenced in an SDLC standard document while the standard document may drive multiple procedure documents that in turn reference multiple standards. Large complex organizations generally have document management systems to help manage this policy complexity. Smaller organizations may have a slimmer document profile.

Document tree for policies, standards, and procedures

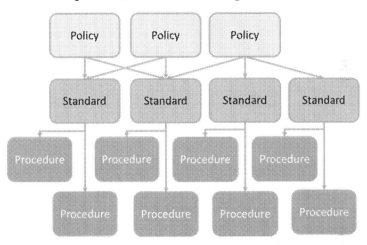

Controls overview

The policies, standards and procedures will be owned by one or more of the roles previously described. These roles are also responsible for establishing controls to help assure that the processes established are operating appropriately. Controls are essential because they serve to ensure that the organization is functioning efficiently, effectively, and in line with guidelines established by the organization. These controls are fundamental to safeguarding the interests of stakeholders, including investors, employees, customers, and the community, by minimizing risks and preventing fraud and misuse of resources.

Financial controls are generally what come to mind when we say controls. These controls help to ensure the accuracy and reliability of financial reporting. They ensure that assets are safeguarded, financial information is recorded accurately, and financial reports are prepared reliably. Additionally, financial controls promote operational efficiency and adherence to prescribed management policies.

Operational controls, on the other hand, provide a structure for effective and efficient decision-making and task execution. They include procedures, standards, and policies designed to ensure the organization operates in a manner that supports its objectives and complies with regulations. These controls encompass a wide range of activities, such as managing risks, optimizing resources, ensuring data integrity, and maintaining the confidentiality of sensitive information.

AI can have controls that can be considered financial or operational depending on the objective of the AI implementation. Controls themselves can be AI as well. An AI system that detects fraud is an example of AI performing a control.

Controls fall into several broad categories: preventative, detective, and corrective.

Preventive controls in the context of artificial intelligence (AI) are proactive measures designed to deter potential problems before they arise. These measures are essential for maintaining the integrity, accuracy, and security of AI systems, and they play a significant role in mitigating risks associated with the development and use of AI technologies. AI preventive controls start at the development phase. Here, they might include the use of robust, diverse datasets to train AI models, helping to reduce bias and improve the fairness of AI outputs. Adequate testing protocols, peer reviews, and quality assurance processes also form part of preventive controls at this stage, ensuring the reliability and accuracy of AI models before deployment.

In terms of data privacy and security, preventive controls might include anonymization of data, robust access controls, and data encryption. These measures are designed to protect sensitive data used or generated by AI systems, mitigating potential data breaches, and ensuring compliance with relevant privacy regulations. Moreover, preventive controls may involve implementing ethical guidelines for AI development and use. This might include the integration of explainability and transparency features into AI models, which can help prevent unintended consequences and foster trust in AI systems.

Training and education form another essential part of preventive controls in AI. Ensuring that all individuals involved in the development and use of AI systems understand the ethical implications, potential risks, and best practices associated with AI can help prevent misuse and unintended consequences.

Detective controls within the realm of AI pertain to mechanisms designed to identify and alert the organization to issues, irregularities, or deviations from expected behavior in AI systems. These controls play a crucial role in risk management by identifying problems promptly, thereby enabling timely corrective action. In the context of AI, detective controls could take various forms. For instance, they might include system monitoring tools that detect anomalies or unusual activity in AI models. These could be patterns that suggest bias in the model's outputs, unexpected shifts in the model's performance, or indicators of potential security threats, such as unauthorized access or data breaches.

Monitoring and reporting systems that track key performance indicators (KPIs) or risk metrics related to AI can also be considered detective controls. These systems might track variables such as the accuracy, fairness, or reliability of AI models, the completeness and quality of data used in AI, or adherence to AI ethics guidelines or regulatory requirements. Furthermore, feedback mechanisms, where users or stakeholders can report issues or concerns about AI systems, are another important type of detective control. These mechanisms can provide valuable insights into how AI systems are performing in real-world conditions and help identify potential problems that may not be evident from system monitoring or audits alone.

Corrective controls in the field of AI refer to the measures taken to address and rectify problems, errors, or irregularities that have been identified in AI systems. These controls are essential for risk management, as they ensure that identified issues are promptly and effectively resolved, thereby preventing further harm, and ensuring the ongoing reliability, security, and ethical use of AI technologies.

In AI systems, corrective controls may involve several forms of action. If a system is found to be producing biased outputs, corrective measures might involve retraining the model with a more diverse dataset, adjusting the model's algorithms, or implementing additional layers of review and quality assurance to mitigate the bias. In cases where a security breach has been identified, corrective controls could include actions such as isolating affected systems, removing unauthorized users, enhancing security protocols, and potentially notifying affected parties in accordance with data breach regulations. Following the immediate response, corrective actions might also involve a review and enhancement of preventative and detective controls to avoid a similar breach in the future. When audits or monitoring systems identify non-compliance with regulations or internal policies, corrective controls may involve updating training programs, revising policies, or enhancing adherence to ethical guidelines. In all cases, corrective controls should also involve a review of the circumstances that led to the non-compliance to prevent recurrence.

Corrective controls in AI often involve feedback loops that allow for continuous improvement. This might include refining AI models based on performance feedback, adjusting governance policies based on lessons learned, or updating risk management strategies based on new insights.

Regardless of the type of controls, they should be auditable. This means that evidence that the control is executed and performing properly exists and can be confirmed by a party separate from the function that owns the control. Typically, internal audit groups validate the operational effectiveness of controls, but other functions could be charged with periodic review.

Controls begin to surface as AI governance frameworks are implemented. There is no one size fits all for controls. AI controls should be risk-based as well as effective and efficient for the goal the control is intended to achieve. Risk and control matrices with tiering regimes are useful for this and exist in many internal audit organizations already use this tool.

Artificial intelligence standards

Anyone can build artificial intelligence applications. The tools are widely available and there is no shortage of websites and tutorials to walk individuals through the development of AI. With the advent of large language models (LLM) and generative AI, AI can now be used to write more AI. As a result of the ubiquitous nature of AI, its use cases have proliferated across industries and functions and rightly so. AI makes human workers more productive and allows them to focus on challenging and more rewarding tasks.

This is similar in nature to how the rise of computer advancements benefited humans. Repetitive tasks were automated and contributed to more efficient and productive processes. Computers enabled humans to perform more complex tasks faster and with greater accuracy. An example that resonates with many in the professional world is the humble spreadsheet. The manual controls, sums and data processing that are now down with this tool keep many businesses running. Much like any tool, however, if it is not used correctly and in a manner that is expected, it won't take much for the tool to become a risk. This is where standards come into play.

To illustrate this, think about the standards that govern driving an automobile in the United States. Traffic rules and licensing guidelines all vary from state to state but it is standard for each state to have traffic laws in place. And, because there are certain standards these laws adhere to, there isn't chaos when moving between jurisdictions. Imagine if no expectation of standards existed for traffic lights. If some states used red lights for stops and others used blue lights while others used yellow, driving across the country would become a lot more difficult and even dangerous. Because there are certain standards such as lights or what stop signs look like, drivers can move about more safely knowing what the expectations are and that other drivers are adhering to similar rules. When drivers are not adhering to the rules, like signaling a turn or making sure a vehicle's lights are in working order, accidents can occur.

Another example that is a little closer to our topic of AI is software development. If an application was coded and sent on its way without adhering to any expectations of meeting user requirements or being thoroughly tested, the application would most likely fail. As a result, many development standards exist that help organizations build software. The classic example is the waterfall methodology where software goes through defined design, build, test and deploy frameworks. Each step along the waterfall journey will have controls and check points as established by the organizational or project need but practitioners know what to generally expect because the standard of this sort of development is well known.

It is arguable that AI is just another software project and can use the same standards. In some cases, this is true. If an organization uses simple machine learning algorithms to forecast revenue, general software and financial controls could suffice for the AI environment. If an organization is running a factory using robotics and optimizing operations using advanced AI algorithms to run just-in-time inventory systems, then a more robust framework catered to AI should be implemented.

This concept is so important that several institutions and governing bodies have established standards or proposed regulations to address the need for governance specific to AI. This is good for organizations implementing AI because it provides an outside perspective from competent experts of what could be in place to make the implementation trustworthy. It also provides frameworks that can be uniformly applied and set expectations of what may be available from one environment to the next. Some of the standards and guidance that have already surfaced in either draft or final form include the Whitehouse AI Bill of Rights, the National Institute of Standards and Technology (NIST) AI Risk Management Framework and ISO 42001:2022.

Each of these standards, and many other standards and laws that are beginning to promulgate, have common themes:

Governance: Policies and procedures provide a framework for the governance of AI systems and enforce the use of policies and procedures that support the responsible management of AI.

Fairness: AI systems should be designed and implemented in a way that avoids unfair bias or discrimination, and address issues such as data bias, algorithmic fairness, and equitable outcomes for different user groups.

Transparent: AI systems should be transparent, meaning the processes and mechanisms underlying their decision-making should be understandable and explainable.

Accountability: Accountability should be promoted in AI systems, ensuring that those responsible for developing and deploying AI technologies can be held accountable for their actions. This includes mechanisms for identifying and addressing the potential harm caused by AI systems.

Privacy and Data Protection: Guidance to emphasize the protection of user data, including anonymization, consent, and secure data handling practices.

Robustness and Reliability: AI systems should be designed to be robust and reliable, capable of performing as intended across different scenarios and environments and should account for issues such as system performance, resilience to adversarial attacks, and the potential for unintended consequences.

Human-Centric Design: AI systems should be developed with a human-centric approach, considering the impact on individuals, society, and the environment.

By adhering to the principles of these themes, practitioners can ensure the AI environment is thoughtfully assessed for risk and that risk mitigation is deliberately developed. Each standard takes a different approach on how to achieve these themes but most of the standards provide guidance on what can be done and/or documented.

Regardless of the standard, the following steps provide guidance on how to take the standard and turn it into actionable steps to implement governance of AI in the organization.

Step 1 – Develop a list of questions to guide the governance review process. Guidance found in each specification of a standard or regulation can be turned into question that the organization should be able to answer. In a later example, we'll see how this can be done. More robust frameworks will generally provide for more questions. When assessing a framework to be used for this effort, do not choose an easy or sparse framework. Do not choose one that is overly restrictive or one that does not fit the organization or industry either. Short of regulation that explicitly specifies what is to be done, the framework chosen should be relevant to the environment in which it will be implemented. Additional considerations when choosing a framework for deriving governance implementation questions include:

What organization sponsors the framework?

Is it widely available?

Is it flexible or prescriptive?

Does the framework provide guidance or is it purely principle based?

Step 2 – Assign owners to each question. Accountability and ownership are the most important aspects of governance. Named individuals with documented accountability are more effective than generalized roles being responsible for high-level outcomes. Having Joan Smith responsible for providing documentation as it relates to disaster recovery is better than having the Director of IT making disaster recovery documents available upon request. The former is easier to audit and track. The latter can become weaker and difficult to manage through time as responsibilities and artifacts change. The owners of questions (and process in general) should also be identified at the appropriate level within the organization. The CEO is theoretically responsible for everything but that is not a name that would be assigned as owner of a detailed task. Conversely, a first-year staff person will not have enough organizational weight to be an owner of a task either. Each organization is different with some having deep hierarchies and others being quite flat so ownership may look different for each organization.

Step 3 – Document responses to each question. Owners assigned to each question document their responses. Responses should seldom be simply yes or no. If an owner feels that the requirement of the question is met, the owner should be able to provide evidence that is auditable by a party outside of their group. For example, a question derived from a framework could be: "*Are there organizational values that address the ethics as it relates to AI?*" An owner could answer "*yes*" and be done but the better answer could be: "Yes. The values deemed to relevant for AI ethics is captured in policy XXX and clearly states there are seven cornerstone values…" The latter answer is auditable and provides supporting evidence. If the response cannot be audited and there is no evidence that can be provided, there is probably a gap.

Step 4 – Perform gap analysis of results to determine project list for gap closure. Once all the questions have been addressed, a list of gaps will develop. Any answer that could be evidence is a gap. Any question that could not be answered is a gap. It is worth mentioning that through the exercise some questions may reveal themselves to be irrelevant. For instance, if an organization is relatively small and only has three applications that are AI, the organization may not need a commercial application to inventory the models. Treatment such as this should be agreed upon and documented by a more senior level of management with an accompanying audit trail that documents the decision.

Step 5 – Prioritize/rationalize list of projects for gap closure. Some gaps are bigger than others with varying degrees of organizational cost. Prioritization is driven by organizational needs but should be risk-based in nature. Gaps that have ethical and safety impacts should take priority over purely administrative gaps. Gaps that are low to no risk may not be addressed by an organization. Each gap should be accompanied by the risks and costs to mitigate so that senior leadership can decide on how best to organize remediation efforts. The list and resulting project plans also provide auditable evidence of implementing the AI governance program.

Step 6 – Audit results of gap analysis and project closure. The audit process can begin early and run parallel up to this point but really begins to have more reportable results at this point in the process. The answers, gaps, and suggested remediation should be reviewed by a team independent of the individuals responsible for implementing the AI governance via this process. This is generally an internal audit team for most organizations, but other specialty groups or external consultants can be used to do the validation and report to senior management.

Step 7 – Report findings and progress to senior leadership. Audit results and potential severity of any findings are reported to senior management by project managers, auditors, and process owners. It is best practice to have a project owner (named individual) see to the coordination and reporting of the overall effort while an audit function opines to the effectiveness of the effort. Example items to report include percent complete of assessment, number of gaps found, percent complete of gap closure, estimated budget impact for closure, and potential issues grouped by severity.

Step 8 - Perform ongoing monitoring of the environment. Status reports for remediation are given to senior managers on a regular basis. Depending on the size of the project or risk, this could be monthly, quarterly, or semi-annually. Additionally, the owners assigned to these items should also be revisited on a periodic basis. As the organization and processes change, so does responsibility and risk. A periodic (annual) confirmation that an owner continues to oversee a particular subject matter is prudent.

The execution of these steps should be managed by a project manager that oversees the coordinated effort. Larger organizations especially need this as some questions may be relevant to multiple individuals in different geographies, departments, etc. Someone will need to coordinate and synthesize responses so that they are mostly uniform. Redundancy and assignment gaps benefit from project management oversight as well. AI is generally considered a technology function so a project manager could be drawn from this function but since governance is more than just technology; risk, legal or other compliance focused group could also host the AI governance implementation project. A temporary group could also be established to drive the effort and report to senior management directly on the progress of the project.

This primer will leverage the NIST AI Risk Management Framework as a guide to implementing AI Governance within an organization. Other frameworks can be used in a similar way provided they contain enough detail. Additionally, some industries do provide regulatory guidance that would need to be considered. Banking and the associated guidance SR11-7 of model risk management is an example of such a scenario.

The NIST AI risk management framework

At the direction of Congress, the National Institute of Standards and Technology (NIST) was commissioned to develop standards for artificial intelligence. The mission, as described by Congress in Title LIII—Department of Commerce Artificial Intelligence Activities is as follows:

1. advance collaborative frameworks, standards, guidelines, and associated methods and techniques for artificial intelligence.
2. support the development of a risk-mitigation framework for deploying artificial intelligence systems.
3. support the development of technical standards and guidelines that promote trustworthy artificial intelligence systems.
4. support the development of technical standards and guidelines by which to test for bias in artificial intelligence training data and applications.

In response, NIST developed the AI Risk Management Framework (AI RMF 1.0). The document describes the importance of AI risk management, defines an AI lifecycle, and provides a framework that can be used to implement or assess an AI environment. The framework consists of four functions that are each supported by several categories and sub-categories. These subcategories address many of the needs for good governance as they apply to the themes described in the last section.

Function	Objective	Sub-categories
Govern	Defines the management processes that should be implemented throughout the AI lifecycle.	19
Map	Defines how AI should be mapped to stakeholders, risks, and capabilities	18
Measure	Defines how quantitative and qualitative measurements should be in place to assess AI implementations	22
Manage	Defines how to address the assignment of resources to risk in the Map and Measure activities as described by policies and procedures established in the Govern function	13

NIST also provided a playbook to accompany the AI RMF. The playbook provides guidance for each of the sub-categories as well as suggested documentation objectives and activities for each of the sub-categories.

The toolset provided by NIST provides a good starter kit for developing governance that addresses AI. The guidance is quite detailed, freely available, and comes with online material that can be integrated into policies, procedures, and audit plans. Subsequent sections of this primer will describe how to take a subcategory from the NIST playbook and perform this integration. Organizations applying the NIST framework as described in the thoughtful manner found in this primer will find that they will be well-positioned to address the risks and complexities of AI as they become more ubiquitous.

The NIST framework is located here:

https://www.nist.gov/itl/ai-risk-management-framework

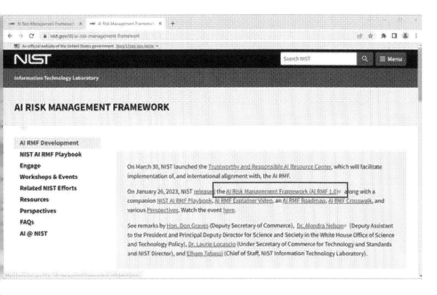

The link in the center of the page is to the framework document. The document NIS AI 100-1 is relatively short at 48 pages. It provides an overview of foundational knowledge around framing risk, the lifecycle of AI, and the categories and subcategories of the framework. The entire document is worth downloading and reading. Section five, AI RMF Core contains the framework categories that are leveraged by this primer to implement AI governance.

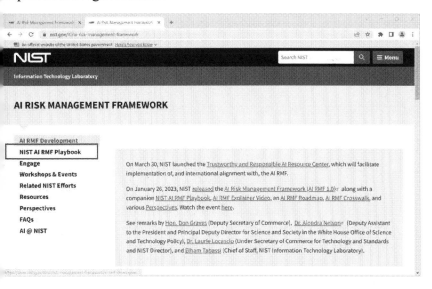

The menu on the left-hand side of the page provides several links. The NIST AI RMF Playbook link will send you to a landing page for the playbook.

At the bottom of the page is a link for the NIST playbook tool.

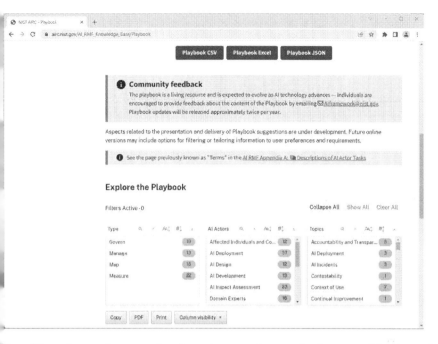

Scrolling down the page leads to interactive tools that provide downloads, printable format, and the ability to filter by specific functions, actors, and topics.

Exploring the playbook via the filters is intuitive. The results of the filters produce a table of the relevant subcategories.

Clicking into the rows reveals the suggested actions and documentation to address the principle of the selected subcategories. These are only suggestions and should not be treated as an exhaustive checklist applicable for every organization. This framework is not compulsory, nor does it satisfy any pre-existing legal requirements. The suggestions can however form the basis of an organizational framework for AI where none may have existed before and help managers, auditors, and developers address risks associated with AI.

The advantage of using the NIST AI RMF and other frameworks is that it forces a deliberate thought process around AI governance that is cross-functional in nature. The NIST framework is a particularly robust a publicly available standards sponsored by a government agency at the time of this writing. Furthermore, as regulatory agencies begin to form laws and rules, they will look to standards such as the NIST AI RMF to inform regulation. AI-enabled entities could benefit by trying to meet future regulations by proactively implementing relevant practices found in these standards sooner rather than later.

If the NIST AI RMF is the framework your organization chooses, it is worth moving beyond this primer and reading the entire framework. Even if NIST is not the framework your organization will use to craft AI governance, it is worth the read. It is free, comprehensive and will likely be an input into future U.S.-based regulation around AI. The categories are reproduced here for a quick reference.

GOVERN

Title	Description
1	**Policies, processes, procedures, and practices across the organization related to the mapping, measuring, and managing of AI risks are in place, transparent, and implemented effectively.**
1.1	Legal and regulatory requirements involving AI are understood, managed, and documented
1.2	The characteristics of trustworthy AI are integrated into organizational policies, processes, and procedures.
1.3	Processes and procedures are in place to determine the needed level of risk management activities based on the organization's risk tolerance.
1.4	The risk management process and its outcomes are established through transparent policies, procedures, and other controls based on organizational risk priorities
1.5	Ongoing monitoring and periodic review of the risk management process and its outcomes are planned, organizational roles and responsibilities are clearly defined, including determining the frequency of periodic review.
1.6	Mechanisms are in place to inventory AI systems and are resourced according to organizational risk priorities
1.7	Processes and procedures are in place for decommissioning and phasing out of AI systems safely and in a manner that does not increase risks or decrease the organization's trustworthiness.
2	**Accountability structures are in place so that the appropriate teams and individuals are empowered, responsible, and trained for mapping, measuring, and managing AI risks.**
2.1	Roles and responsibilities and lines of communication related to mapping, measuring, and managing AI risks are documented and are clear to individuals and teams throughout the organization.

2.2	The organization's personnel and partners receive AI risk management training to enable them to perform their duties and responsibilities consistent with related policies, procedures, and agreements.
2.3	Executive leadership of the organization takes responsibility for decisions about risks associated with AI system development and deployment.
3	**Workforce diversity, equity, inclusion, and accessibility processes are prioritized in the mapping, measuring, and managing of AI risks throughout the lifecycle.**
3.1	Decision-makings related to mapping, measuring, and managing AI risks throughout the lifecycle is informed by a diverse team (e.g., diversity of demographics, disciplines, experience, expertise, and backgrounds).
3.2	Policies and procedures are in place to define and differentiate roles and responsibilities for human-AI configurations and oversight of AI systems
4	**Organizational teams are committed to a culture that considers and communicates AI risk.**
4.1	Organizational policies, and practices are in place to foster a critical thinking and safety-first mindset in the design, development, deployment, and uses of AI systems to minimize negative impacts
4.2	Organizational teams document the risks and potential impacts of the AI technology they design, develop, deploy, evaluate, and use, and communicate about the impacts more broadly
4.3	Organizational practices are in place to enable AI testing, identification of incidents, and information sharing.
5	**Processes are in place for robust engagement with relevant AI actors.**
5.1	Organizational policies and practices are in place to collect, consider, prioritize, and integrate feedback from those external to the team that developed or deployed the AI system regarding the potential individual and societal impacts related to AI risks.
5.2	Mechanisms are established to enable AI actors to regularly incorporate adjudicated feedback from relevant AI actors into system design and implementation.

6	**Policies and procedures are in place to address AI risks and benefits arising from third-party software and data and other supply chain issues.**
6.1	Policies and procedures are in place that address AI risks associated with third-party entities, including risks of infringement of a third party's intellectual property or other rights.
6.2	Contingency processes are in place to handle failures or incidents in third-party data or AI systems deemed to be high-risk.

MAP

Title	Description
1	**Context is established and understood.**
1.1	Intended purpose, potentially beneficial uses, context-specific laws, norms and expectations, and prospective settings in which the AI system will be deployed are understood and documented. Considerations include: specific set or types of users along with their expectations; potential positive and negative impacts of system uses to individuals, communities, organizations, society, and the planet; assumptions and related limitations about AI system purposes; uses and risks across the development or product AI lifecycle; TEVV and system metrics.
1.2	Inter-disciplinary AI actors, competencies, skills, and capacities for establishing context reflect demographic diversity and broad domain and user experience expertise, and their participation is documented. Opportunities for interdisciplinary collaboration are prioritized.
1.3	The organization's mission and relevant goals for the AI technology are understood and documented.
1.4	The business value or context of business use has been clearly defined or – in the case of assessing existing AI systems – re-evaluated.
1.5	Organizational risk tolerances are determined and documented.
1.6	System requirements (e.g., "the system shall respect the privacy of its users") are elicited from and understood by relevant AI actors. Design decisions take socio-technical implications into account to address AI risks.
2	**Categorization of the AI system is performed.**

41

2.1	The specific task, and methods used to implement the task, that the AI system will support is defined (e.g., classifiers, generative models, recommenders).
2.2	Information about the AI system's knowledge limits and how system output may be utilized and overseen by humans is documented. Documentation provides sufficient information to assist relevant AI actors when making informed decisions and taking subsequent actions.
2.3	Scientific integrity and TEVV considerations are identified and documented, including those related to experimental design, data collection and selection (e.g., availability, representativeness, suitability), system trustworthiness, and construct validation.
3	**AI capabilities, targeted usage, goals, and expected benefits and costs compared with appropriate benchmarks are understood.**
3.1	Potential benefits of intended AI system functionality and performance are examined and documented.
3.2	Potential costs, including non-monetary costs, which result from expected or realized AI errors or system functionality and trustworthiness - as connected to organizational risk tolerance - are examined and documented.
3.3	Targeted application scope is specified and documented based on the system's capability, established context, and AI system categorization.
3.4	Processes for operator and practitioner proficiency with AI system performance and trustworthiness – and relevant technical standards and certifications – are defined, assessed, and documented.
3.5	Processes for human oversight are defined, assessed, and documented in accordance with organizational policies from GOVERN function.
4	**Risks and benefits are mapped for all components of the AI system including third-party software and data.**
4.1	Approaches for mapping AI technology and legal risks of its components – including the use of third-party data or software – are in place, followed, and documented, as are risks of infringement of a third-party's intellectual property or other rights.
4.2	Internal risk controls for components of the AI system including third-party AI technologies are identified and documented.

	Impacts to individuals, groups, communities, organizations, and society are characterized.
5	
5.1	Likelihood and magnitude of each identified impact (both potentially beneficial and harmful) based on expected use, past uses of AI systems in similar contexts, public incident reports, feedback from those external to the team that developed or deployed the AI system, or other data are identified and documented.
5.2	Practices and personnel for supporting regular engagement with relevant AI actors and integrating feedback about positive, negative, and unanticipated impacts are in place and documented.

MEASURE

Title	Description
1	**Appropriate methods and metrics are identified and applied.**
1.1	Approaches and metrics for measurement of AI risks enumerated during the Map function are selected for implementation starting with the most significant AI risks. The risks or trustworthiness characteristics that will not – or cannot – be measured are properly documented.
1.2	Appropriateness of AI metrics and effectiveness of existing controls is regularly assessed and updated including reports of errors and impacts on affected communities.
1.3	Internal experts who did not serve as front-line developers for the system and/or independent assessors are involved in regular assessments and updates. Domain experts, users, AI actors external to the team that developed or deployed the AI system, and affected communities are consulted in support of assessments as necessary per organizational risk tolerance.
2	**AI systems are evaluated for trustworthy characteristics.**
2.1	Test sets, metrics, and details about the tools used during test, evaluation, validation, and verification (TEVV) are documented.
2.2	Evaluations involving human subjects meet applicable requirements (including human subject protection) and are representative of the relevant population.
2.3	AI system performance or assurance criteria are measured qualitatively or quantitatively and demonstrated for conditions like deployment setting(s). Measures are documented.

43

2.4	The functionality and behavior of the AI system and its components – as identified in the MAP function – are monitored when in production.
2.5	The AI system to be deployed is demonstrated to be valid and reliable. Limitations of the generalizability beyond the conditions under which the technology was developed are documented.
2.6	AI system is evaluated regularly for safety risks – as identified in the MAP function. The AI system to be deployed is demonstrated to be safe, its residual negative risk does not exceed the risk tolerance, and can fail safely, particularly if made to operate beyond its knowledge limits. Safety metrics implicate system reliability and robustness, real-time monitoring, and response times for AI system failures.
2.7	AI system security and resilience – as identified in the MAP function – are evaluated and documented.
2.8	Risks associated with transparency and accountability – as identified in the MAP function – are examined and documented.
2.9	The AI model is explained, validated, and documented, and AI system output is interpreted within its context – as identified in the MAP function – and to inform responsible use and governance.
2.1	Privacy risk of the AI system – as identified in the MAP function – is examined and documented.
2.11	Fairness and bias – as identified in the MAP function – is evaluated and results are documented.
2.12	Environmental impact and sustainability of AI model training and management activities – as identified in the MAP function – are assessed and documented.
2.13	Effectiveness of the employed TEVV metrics and processes in the MEASURE function are evaluated and documented.
3	**Mechanisms for tracking identified AI risks over time are in place.**
3.1	Approaches, personnel, and documentation are in place to regularly identify and track existing, unanticipated, and emergent AI risks based on factors such as intended and actual performance in deployed contexts.
3.2	Risk tracking approaches are considered for settings where AI risks are difficult to assess using currently available measurement techniques or where metrics are not yet available.
3.3	Feedback processes for end users and impacted communities to report problems and appeal system outcomes are established and integrated into AI system evaluation metrics.

44

4	**Feedback about efficacy of measurement is gathered and assessed.**
4.1	Measurement approaches for identifying AI risks are connected to deployment context(s) and informed through consultation with domain experts and other end users. Approaches are documented.
4.2	Measurement results regarding AI system trustworthiness in deployment context(s) and across AI lifecycle are informed by input from domain experts and other relevant AI actors to validate whether the system is performing consistently as intended. Results are documented.
4.3	Measurable performance improvements or declines based on consultations with relevant AI actors including affected communities, and field data about context-relevant risks and trustworthiness characteristics, are identified and documented.

MANAGE

Title	Description
1	**AI risks based on assessments and other analytical output from the MAP and MEASURE functions are prioritized, responded to, and managed.**
1.1	A determination is as to whether the AI system achieves its intended purpose and stated objectives and whether its development or deployment should proceed.
1.2	Treatment of documented AI risks is prioritized based on impact, likelihood, or available resources or methods.
1.3	Responses to the AI risks deemed high priority as identified by the Map function, are developed, planned, and documented. Risk response options can include mitigating, transferring, avoiding, or accepting.
1.4	Negative residual risks (defined as the sum of all unmitigated risks) to both downstream acquirers of AI systems and end users are documented.
2	**Strategies to maximize AI benefits and minimize negative impacts are planned, prepared, implemented, documented, and informed by input from relevant AI actors.**
2.1	Resources required to manage AI risks are considered, along with viable non-AI alternative systems, approaches, or methods – to reduce the magnitude or likelihood of potential impacts.

2.2	Mechanisms are in place and applied to sustain the value of deployed AI systems.
2.3	Procedures are followed to respond to and recover from a previously unknown risk when it is identified.
2.4	Mechanisms are in place and applied, responsibilities are assigned and understood to supersede, disengage, or deactivate AI systems that demonstrate performance or outcomes inconsistent with intended use.
3	**AI risks and benefits from third-party entities are managed.**
3.1	AI risks and benefits from third-party resources are regularly monitored, and risk controls are applied and documented.
3.2	Pre-trained models which are used for development are monitored as part of AI system regular monitoring and maintenance.
4	**Risk treatments, including response and recovery, and communication plans for the identified and measured AI risks are documented and monitored regularly.**
4.1	Post-deployment AI system monitoring plans are implemented, including mechanisms for capturing and evaluating input from users and other relevant AI actors, appeal and override, decommissioning, incident response, recovery, and change management.
4.2	Measurable activities for continual improvements are integrated into AI system updates and include regular engagement with interested parties, including relevant AI actors.
4.3	Incidents and errors are communicated to relevant AI actors including affected communities. Processes for tracking, responding to, and recovering from incidents and errors are followed and documented.

Walkthrough

The categories in the previous section could by themselves help drive the development of an organizational governance framework that addresses AI. Professionals within governance, risk, and audit functions could analyze these and derive policies, standards, and controls that address each item listed. This list should not be considered a definitive checklist, however. Industry and organizational factors as well as regulatory constraints need to be addressed as well. This framework helps to provide guidance on how an organization could review its internal AI governance and discover any gaps that may exist.

As mentioned earlier, each subcategory comes with additional guidance that could help shape AI governance or assess any gaps. We'll use GOVERN subcategory 1.2 to demonstrate how this can be accomplished with a walkthrough. This subcategory provides substantial guidance within the playbook that can be used for assessment.

Following the tutorial in the previous section on how to obtain detailed information from the NIST playbook will provide us with suggested actions and/or documentation that address the objective of the subcategory. First, let us review the objective of GOVERN subcategory 1.2.

"Policies, processes, and procedures are central components of effective AI risk management and fundamental to individual and organizational accountability. All stakeholders benefit from policies, processes, and procedures which require preventing harm by design and default.

Organizational policies and procedures will vary based on available resources and risk profiles, but can help systematize AI actor roles and responsibilities throughout the AI lifecycle. Without such policies, risk management can be subjective across the organization, and exacerbate rather than minimize risks over time. Polices, or summaries thereof, are understandable to relevant AI actors. Policies reflect an understanding of the underlying metrics, measurements, and tests that are necessary to support policy and AI system design, development, deployment, and use.

Lack of clear information about responsibilities and chains of command will limit the effectiveness of risk management."

This subcategory focuses on policies and documentation which is the cornerstone of any governance. Policies remove subjectivity from procedures and ownership and help define how actions should be articulated and executed. Organizational policies drive organizational standards which in turn drive organizational procedures. Policies generally are a set of inter-related documents that have specific owners. Some large organizations have a hierarchy of policies that may be numerous in nature but very focused. Other organizations have very lengthy policies that can act almost like procedures. The guidance provided here does not address what your policies should look like since that is driven by the individual organization. This will address what should be considered within the policies to address AI governance.

We can now look at the suggested actions to determine if our current governance framework has sufficiently addressed the objectives of the subcategory or if there are any potential gaps. As we said earlier, this is not a definitive checklist but going through the exercise of reviewing the suggested actions and documentation promotes a discipline review of the AI environment. The suggested actions from the playbook for this subcategory is as follows:

1. Define key terms and concepts related to AI systems and the scope of their purposes and intended uses.
2. Connect AI governance to existing organizational governance and risk controls.
3. Align to broader data governance policies and practices, particularly the use of sensitive or otherwise risky data.
4. Detail standards for experimental design, data quality, and model training.
5. Outline and document risk mapping and measurement processes and standards.
6. Detail model testing and validation processes.
7. Detail review processes for legal and risk functions.
8. Establish the frequency of and detail for monitoring, auditing, and review processes.
9. Outline change management requirements.
10. Outline processes for internal and external stakeholder engagement.

11. Establish whistleblower policies to facilitate reporting of serious AI system concerns.
12. Detail and test incident response plans.
13. Verify that formal AI risk management policies align to existing legal standards, and industry best practices and norms.
14. Establish AI risk management policies that broadly align to AI system trustworthy characteristics.
15. Verify that formal AI risk management policies include currently deployed and third-party AI systems.

We'll go through a few of these at a high level in the following example to demonstrate the process of performing an assessment and gap analysis for AI governance. To do this, we'll turn each suggested item into one or more questions and provide some potential guidance.

1. Define key terms and concepts related to AI systems and the scope of their purposes and intended uses.

This can be turned into several questions that may have different owners:

1.1 – Are key terms and concepts related to AI systems documented?

Definitions for AI can be found in a policy or departmental procedure. The owner of this question may be a technology manager or functional manager. The terms may include what the organization considers AI and the names of substantial AI systems used throughout the organization.

1.2 – Is the scope, purpose and intended use for each implementation documented?

Each AI model should have a document associated with it. In the documentation, there should be a section about what the model achieved and why. For example: "Model XYZ is a K-nearest neighbor (KNN) model that uses sales data gathered from web traffic for product A's web page to determine significant demographic groups that can be used to drive marketing campaigns." This description provides a little amount the method, the data and how the results are used. Details may be more descriptive and will evolve over time.

2. Is AI governance connected to existing organizational governance and risk controls?

Most organizations have a set of policies that reference each other and are managed at a high-level in a similar fashion. Human Resource policies and Finance policies are different, but they are managed in a similar manner utilizing policy owners, evidence of reviews and periodic audits. AI policies are no different. The control framework related to AI should also be managed in a similar fashion. For those who are familiar with SOX, we can think of AI controls as special purpose SOX controls. If there is a control management platform in place, AI controls should be included in it. Like these questions and every other organizational control, AI controls should have an owner that can provide evidence the control is in place and working.

3. Does AI data governance align to broader data governance policies and practices, particularly the use of sensitive or otherwise risky data?

Where possible, it is a good practice to leverage existing policies. Companies that are sophisticated enough to need AI governance will most likely have data policies in place. AI policies should document linkage to data policies explicitly. All data controls, owners, practices, etc. that are documented for data governance apply to AI. In the instances where there is deviation, this would be documented in a specific AI policy. Data policy owners should be included in the data discussion if they are not already the owners of the AI-specific data policies.

4. Are there detailed standards for experimental design, data quality, and model training?

AI policy documents should require that standards for development exist. The standards would indicate the framework of what must be addressed (like this document). Each AI model would then in turn be built in accordance with the standards and its own model document and/or procedure that evidences this compliance. For example, policy ABC would state that each model must be built in accordance with standard LMN as owned and maintained by the designated group (Tech, Risk, other functional group). The group would then evidence the compliance with the documented standards via a model document, test results or other evidence. The policies and standards should be flexible enough to address the varying types of models within the organization. A forecasting model and classification model may have different types of data and testing requirements but the need for testing and evidence of testing does not change even if the type of testing does differ.

5. Are the risk mapping and measurement processes and standards documented?

AI implementation risk identification process should align with the existing organizational risk mapping process. If a risk identification process does not exist for the organization, then one specific to AI could be created. The MAP function in the NIST framework provides some guidance on how to do this but an example could be a process where identified stakeholders identify risks that may map to financial, reputational, or other risks in a quarterly review session. The process and the details of the expected outcomes, e.g., risk with associated potentials loss metric, could be documented to meet this goal.

In the above example, there are 15 topics that cover one of the 72 subcategories within the NIST framework. Not all the subcategories have guidance that is this verbose, but all categories do provide guidance that can be turned into actionable assessments. Utilizing the framework in this manner makes it a comprehensive guide for addressing AI governance.

Other frameworks have similar structure and most regulatory requirements can be broken down this way as well. ISO 42001:2022 mentioned earlier has number of similar categories to the NIST framework that each provide potential controls and guidance. As a form of best practices, multiple frameworks could be utilized simultaneously to ensure comprehensive coverage for AI governance. A matrix can be created to align questions and owners with guidance from multiple frameworks. This can be useful in a regulatory environment where there are standards as well as specific rules that must be addressed.

Sample Matrix

	Standard 1	Standard 2	Regulation 1
Does the organization have policy that defines roles and responsibilities?	X	NA	X
Are key metrics related compliance filed in the specified format?	NA	NA	X

Once the relevant framework questions have been developed and agreed upon, the owners can respond to them, and the responses can be gathered. Potential owners have been provided in the example, but the NIST framework also provides potential owners. In the example above using GOVERN 1.2, NIST describes the actors as "Governance and Oversight." These actors are further defined broadly in the NIST framework as "organizational management, senior leadership, and the Board of Directors." Each organization will have different roles that may take on AI responsibilities but if there is some trouble in defining which role could own a topic, the NIST framework provides suggestions that can help an organization home in on the proper owner. It is best practice that the ultimate owner has a role and that the individual currently in the role is named.

After the questions are answered AND evidence is provided, gaps should be listed, and the results should be turned over to audit for review as per the recommended project flow found in the Artificial Intelligence Standards section of this primer. From here it is project management to identify and close gaps and work with stakeholders to communicate status of the implementation project.

Another artifact of the project should be the key controls associated with the questions that were addressed by a stakeholder. Controls can be in the form of signoffs, automated procedures, notifications, etc. These controls should appear alongside other controls in the organization and be managed in a similar fashion. Each question or item addressed may not have their own unique control, but a control can address more than one item. Conversely, an item may need more than one key control. We can use GOVERN category 1 as an example.

Title	Subcategory	Potential Control
1.1	Legal and regulatory requirements involving AI are understood, managed, and documented	Regulatory review of documented AI regulations is performed each quarter by Legal department and is evidenced via summary sent to Chief AI Officer who provides sign-off.
1.2	The characteristics of trustworthy AI are integrated into organizational policies, processes, and procedures.	AI policy exists and evidences annual review and sign-off by owners who attest to the completeness of the policy.
1.3	Processes and procedures are in place to determine the needed level of risk management activities based on the organization's risk tolerance.	
1.4	The risk management process and its outcomes are established through transparent policies, procedures, and other controls based on organizational risk priorities	AI risk management activities is included in corporate risk procedure XYZ which is executed on annual basis to document and quantify organizational risk.
1.5	Ongoing monitoring and periodic review of the risk management process and its outcomes are planned, organizational roles and responsibilities are clearly defined, including determining the frequency of periodic review.	
1.6	Mechanisms are in place to inventory AI systems and are resourced according to organizational risk priorities	AI policy requires an inventory of all systems designated as AI to be maintained by the Chief AI Officer and certified on an annual basis.
1.7	Processes and procedures are in place for decommissioning and phasing out of AI systems safely and in a manner that does not increase risks or decrease the organization's trustworthiness.	AI development standard requires each AI implementation to contain decommissioning procedures within the implementations documentation.

Audit would periodically test these controls at an organizational or implementation level and provide feedback.

Summary

AI is still maturing as a capability in most organizations. With the advent of generative AI, it is becoming more of a topic in board meetings, internal audit groups, and the media. The guidance in this primer will not solve or identify all problems that will arise in this new space. However, by following this guidance, regardless of the framework chosen, organizations will be better placed to meet the new challenges as well as emerging regulations.

Acknowledgements

Special thanks to my Editor in Chief and wife Amy Hayden for making this primer and me better one comment at time.

Printed in France by Amazon
Brétigny-sur-Orge, FR

17192094R00033